AN UNFORESEEABLE CHANGE:

The Story of Norman Lee Brown

David Swarbrick

TotalRecall Publications, Inc.
1103 Middlecreek
Friendswood, Texas 77546
281-992-3131 281-482-5390 Fax
www.totalrecallpress.com

All rights reserved. Except as permitted under the United States Copyright Act of 1976, No part of this publication may be reproduced, stored in a retrieval system, or transmitted in any form or by any means electronic or mechanical or by photocopying, recording, or otherwise without prior permission of the publisher. Exclusive worldwide content publication / distribution by TotalRecall Publications, Inc.

Copyright © 2016 by David Swarbrick
All rights reserved

ISBN: 978-1-59095-552-9
UPC: 6-43977-45528-4

Printed in the United States of America with simultaneous printing in Australia, Canada, and United Kingdom.

FIRST EDITION
1 2 3 4 5 6 7 8 9 10

The scanning, uploading and distribution of this book via the Internet or via any other means without the permission of the publisher is illegal and punishable by law. Please purchase only authorized electronic editions, and do not participate in or encourage electronic piracy of copyrighted materials. Your support of the author's rights is appreciated.

This book is dedicated to anyone and everyone who has had to endure the long and tough struggle of dealing with someone close to them, or losing someone close to them due to a chemical dependency problem. To those, I offer my deepest sympathies. Just always remember… you're not alone.

I also thank you for purchasing this book. I hope when you read it to your children, or if they read it on their own, that one of you, if not all of you, learn something from it.

Sincerely
David E. Swarbrick…
www.davidswarbrick.webs.com

About The Book

An Unforeseeable Change: The Story of Norman Lee Brown, is a short story loosely based on my own personal experiences, and careful observations of everyday things that continually take place around me. Narrated by me, the author, it shows and tells in a very straightforward manner the profound truths about what can actually happen to kids, dreams, families, and society when teenagers use/experiment with drugs. Meant for most ages, it should make you laugh, cry, think, and hopefully most of all, it will educate you. Now, I know that some of you at this moment who are reading, are probably thinking or saying to yourselves,

Oh, whoopdy-do! Another book written by an angry old man about substance abuse, in which it was only created for the specific intent to target younger generations! Boring… they're all the same. And how many times has it been done?

Well, this one's not the same. That wasn't my intent, and as long as our species is continually plagued by an ever-growing epidemic that is infecting all of us, our whole being, right down to our spirit, and livelihoods, these books and stories have to be written and repeatedly told. Hopefully for the human race, right up until the very day that this outright, ridiculous, atrocity wishfully comes to an end, and beyond it, such stories will be.

In all of the great gifts given to us at the time of our conception, and to the glorious path that awaits us, in this life, all it takes is one bad choice to have these gifts taken away, and to forever be removed from our true path. From the very moment you were created, you were given something extraordinary. That something extraordinary is life, and within that life given, you, and everyone all around you, no matter who you are, was also given another kind of special gift. This special gift was planted deep inside you, and for some, there are multiple gifts. Now, while you were carefully shaped and formed within your mother's womb, a natural talent of some sort, and the remarkable abilities to carry out with this talent throughout your life was placed upon you. A talent and ability that serves nearly an incomprehensible purpose, which when discovered and properly nurtured, will slowly grow with you throughout your life, and eventually blossom into a beautiful, eternal flower. Just always remember this, and forever carry it with you: You are special. You are divine, and your life means something. So don't waste it, and don't throw your gifts, life, and talents away to drugs.

1

Not to long ago, on a warm spring evening, Norman Lee Brown was born. He was born into the universe to a mother and father who were so excited, and had loved him oh so much. To them, having Norman was like a dream come true, and from the very beginning he was always a good and extremely bright child. As a baby he never really fussed too much. As a toddler he was always happy and playful, and as a little boy in early school, Norman was generally a good student, and pretty much a pleasant person to be around. He got good grades. Had a lot of friends. He was respectful, eventful, polite, and always willing to help others when he was needed. Helping with specific things, such as others with their homework, his parents with household chores, and the elderly with tasks that they normally couldn't do on their own.

Shortly on, Norman learned that sometimes he could earn money from doing these things, which to him was really cool and fun. Cool, because Norman liked earning money and saving up to buy the things he wanted. And it was fun because Norman enjoyed helping out, and he also loved to be around the people that he helped, mainly his family.

Norman loved and cherished his family. His mom, dad, aunts, uncles, cousins, grandparents, and close friends meant everything to him. Norman meant everything to them equally as well, and along with his parents, they were all always very supportive of most everything he did. Just like every growing and developing child though, Norman did have the occasional problem with slightly misbehaving and not listening very well. But it was never really too serious, and those things were to be expected. Often with Norman the incidents were far and few between, most times resolved quickly, and it had always seemed as though Norman had learned something from whatever the ordeal had been, and it usually never occurred again.

Whenever his parents or elders sat him down to explain something, and how his behavior wasn't acceptable, Norman most generally and very respectfully listened.

Sometimes it took more than once, though. Like one time when he was just 6 years old

2

It was a Friday afternoon. Norman had been home from school for a while, and his dad had just gotten home from work. He said, "Hi," to, Norman, visited with him for a moment, and after the short visit, he explained that he had to help mom get dinner ready, and that Norman should play in his room until called. He was told to do so, because while mom and dad are cooking, the kitchen can be a very dangerous place for little ones. Norman carefully listened, and politely said when his dad was done speaking,

"Okay."

Norman's dad then went off to help with dinner, and Norman went off to his room. He began to peacefully keep himself occupied with some toys. Shortly after though, he got bored, and wanted to have some fun. He didn't quite understand why he had to stay in his room, so he stopped what he was doing, ran out of his room, through a hallway, and into the kitchen. He started to dance, scream, yell, and bounce wildly around the room. Norman's mother tripped over him, and she was carrying a pot of boiling water. She almost spilled it all over Norman, which would have seriously injured him.

Quickly, Norman's dad reacted, "Norman Lee!" He said in a strong, stern voice, "Off to your room, young man! Now!"

Norman immediately stopped, looked at his dad, then to his mother. Silence fell across the room, and Norman walked off to his bedroom. Norman's dad followed, and his mother continued on with dinner. Though he didn't mean it, and he was only trying to have fun, Norman knew by the tone of his dad's voice, and the look of horror across his mother's face, that he should have done what his dad had told him to do.

When Norman was instructed to stay and play in his room, and his dad explained why, it was for a very, very good reason.

When the two of them reached his room, Norman's dad carefully explained all of this to him again. He also calmly told him of the possible outcome if the pot of boiling water had gotten spilled on him. Norman didn't like the sound of that. So he thought for a moment, and then fully understood why he shouldn't be in the kitchen while his mom, dad, or adults are cooking. He said,

"I'm sorry, dad. It won't happen again."

"It's okay." Norman's dad replied with a smile, "I'm just glad you didn't get hurt, and I'm sure mom's glad, too. Now go play until we call on you."

With that said, Norman's dad left the room, and went back to the kitchen.

Norman got some toys and began to peacefully play while he waited for dinner, and he never again, until he was older went into the kitchen while mom, dad, or adults were cooking.

3

Throughout the years, Norman grew and developed as a child would be expected to, and for most parents who wish their children would stay little forever, to his mom and dad's dismay, Norman grew up. One day he was born, the next he was a preteen, and soon he reached adolescences. To Norman's mom, dad, and family, it seemed as though time had flown by.

Norman's parents would often reminisce together about his early childhood, and sometimes they would tell and tease Norman about some of the cute, silly little things that he often did when he was younger. This would usually embarrass him, and he would just walk away blushing. His parents didn't mean anything negative towards Norman by their little teases. They just loved him a lot, and the two of them enjoyed sharing the things with him that he had done and had no memory of doing.

One of their favorites to tell, and his grandparents as well, was when Norman was about 3 years old.

It was a warm, beautiful, summer day. The sun was out, and there wasn't but only a few puffy white clouds hanging in the deep blue sky. Norman's mom and dad had a few friends and a few family members over for an afternoon dinner. Norman wandered out to the garage for a moment, and quickly came back in carrying a partially broken, child-sized fishing pole. The fishing pole was a complete rod and reel, made especially for small children, and the tip had been broken off. Now, at this point in Norman's life, he couldn't quite pronounce his words correctly. As it is with most children his age, he would get his,

P's, T's, H's, and F's mixed up, which was generally pretty cute-sounding when he first began to speak, and don't deny it, but at one time in our lives, we all did it. So, when Norman came back in, he went to his grandpa, who was sitting at the kitchen table with his mom, dad, and grandmother. He showed him the broken fishing pole, and innocently said,

"Papa, look; I broke my pissing pole, pissing in duh garage."

That really struck everyone in the room as being funny, and they all immediately began to laugh. As did Norman, though he didn't know what was so funny. He giggled and laughed, too. Norman's grandpa responded while he, himself slowed his laughter to a jolly little giggle,

"Aw, you did, huh? Well, papa's gonna just have to buy you a new one."

"Mm, hmm…" Norman simply replied as he shook his head, and said, "Den we can go pissing in duh garage together."

Everyone in the room, including Norman and his grandpa, laughed even harder when, Norman said that.

"Well, I don't know about pissing with you in the garage, Son." Norman's grandpa responded through his own laughter, "But we can go fishing together at a nice big lake. What do you say?"

"Otay!" Norman replied cheerfully loud, "Me and Papa are gonna go pissing together!"

With that said, the laughter continued, and Norman walked off carrying the fishing pole, laughing as well.

How cute and totally innocent that whole thing was. It's those little moments in our lives that make it special, and well worth living to it's fullest. One can see why it's one of Norman's mom, dad, and family's favorite stories about him to tell. He was always very entertaining, and just as all of us are, was a very special little person.

During the time of his mother's pregnancy though, little known to his parents and family, when Mother Nature carefully began forming Norman within his mother's womb, a talent from the far, far reaches of the cosmos was placed deep inside of him. As is with everyone, including you, Norman was given the great gift of life. He was also given another gift that, within a year and a half of his mother giving birth to him, would soon be discovered.

4

Shortly after Norman was able to sit up on his own, his parents took very curious notice to something he would do, and which he would do quite often. Most times it would be when he was in his highchair waiting to be fed, being fed, or feeding himself. Other times it would be when he was just simply sitting somewhere. Whether it be in his playpen, in his car seat, in the bathtub, or in the living room on the floor playing with his toys, Norman would innocently tap his hands and little fingers on things like he was playing the drums. His mom and dad at times would quietly watch him do this, and they would deeply wonder about it. They would wonder because, as we all know, most little ones will go through a stage in which they like to pound their hands, fingers, feet, or whatever they can get their hands on, on random things, and it just sounds like noise. They even go through a period of throwing things. But with Norman, his parents, and close family would wonder because he wasn't just making noise. Norman was creating syncopation's, time signatures, and keeping simple beats all without the aid of hearing music, or obviously being able to read it.

When he was in his highchair with his little silverware, Norman would use the silverware as though they were drumsticks, and when he wasn't filling his face, he would drum on the various things in front of him.

Marveling at what appeared to be something truly extraordinary, Norman's mom and dad often encouraged him, steered him towards the drumming, and they bought him his first little drum set when he was just 4 years old. Norman progressed on that set very rapidly, and throughout his growing years, without forcing it upon him, Norman's parents continued to encourage and lightly surround him with music.

Eventually when Norman was a little older they got him a full-sized drum set, which he mastered in only a few hours, and soon after, because his dad was a part-time musician, Norman quickly learned other instruments as well. He learned the six-string guitar. The four-string bass, the keyboard, and the xylophone. He learned the xylophone in his school band class, and he also wasn't too bad of a singer, either.

Sometimes he would sit in and play shows for people with his dad. His first one was when he was only 7, and though all one could see was the top of a young boy's head peeking out from the top of the drum set, people loved it. Those who saw him play, or knew him personally, were completely amazed by his abilities. Abilities and skills that would have taken most people half their lifetime to master, Norman had mastered at a very young age, and in an unheard of amount of time.

His natural drumming, and nearly effortless musical talents were truly remarkable, and a very beautiful thing. Norman's dad, along with his mother, had often dreamed of recording an album with him, and one day touring the world together as a power-house father-and-son act. Norman too, dreamed of these things. He also imagined that he would eventually make music his life. But before any of this could happen, Norman had to be a kid first, and his parents, family, and close friends made sure of it. Though he was a little musical prodigy, and started his very own first band when he was just 12, Norman still had to go to school, grow, learn, and develop in the natural ways a child is meant to. There would be plenty of time later on in life to do these other things.

Those early times for Norman and his family, were truly wonderful times. The house was always full of love, laughter, music, and togetherness. It was almost magical, and it had seemed that all good things had been laid out before them. Mainly for Norman. The universe had given him a great gift, a great family, and had also laid out an awesome path for him to follow. Music was Norman's true destiny. But in order to fulfill this destiny, he would have to work hard at it, hard in school, and stay on the right path.

Sometime around the ages of 13 and 14, though, Norman did go through that little teenage rebellion stage we've all gone through. He momentarily steered off his path for a bit, slacked off in school, and was slightly disrespectful to people around him, which caused a few minor arguments between him and his parents. But nothing too serious, and the arguments were generally over with as soon as they began. Unfortunately this happens with a lot of teens. It's to be expected, and for most, it doesn't last very long. Thankfully for Norman and his family, it didn't last too long for him, either. Shortly before he turned 15 the whole stage had just seemed to disappear, and Norman got back on track. He stopped slacking off in school, toned his disrespectfulness down, and in his spare time he continued on with creating music. All things were looking good, and it seemed Norman had a very bright future ahead of him.

5

A few days before Normans 16th birthday, he went out with his friend, Mark. It was a Saturday night, Mark was old enough to drive, and he had gotten the use of his brother's car. Norman had finished up his homework the night before, he wasn't creating any music at the time, and he really had nothing to do. Plus, he really wanted to go out with Mark. Mark had just recently gotten his driver's license, and all they had been talking about was going out some night for a while, simply driving around. Norman's parents, generally very easy-going, and never ones to over-enforce too many rules on Norman, were fine with it. As long as he was home before midnight and tried to stay out of trouble, which Norman was also never really one to get into any trouble, and his parents knew this. But being parents, it was their job to remind him not to. Norman knew this as well. So, he respectfully listened to them, and said, when Mark arrived at his house,

"Okay, thanks, and I'll be seeing you."

"Bye, and have fun." Norman's parents responded smiling.

"Will do." Norman happily replied as he walked out of the house.

6

Sometime into their drive, Norman and Mark stopped at a convenience store to get a couple of sodas. Inside the store, they ran into a few people that they knew from school. One of them told Mark and Norman about a small party that was gathering together not too far away at an old abandoned warehouse out off the side of desolate dirt road, and that they should go and check it out. "Sure, why not, and what'll it hurt?" The two of them decided after they momentarily talked about whether they should go or not, "We just won't stay long, and we'll have plenty of time to keep driving around."

A little while later, they arrived at the abandoned warehouse, got out of the car, and made their way inside. On their way, the two of them eyed a couple of cars that were parked around the building, and they could also hear faint music coming from the inside. Norman immediately started air drumming to the sound, and Mark just looked at him, laughed, and shook his head. He asked,

"You just can't ever stop, can you?"

"Nope." Norman replied with a serious looking grin, "Most of the time, I can't. But, sometimes I'm willing to make an exception."

"Well, right now, you need to make that exception." Mark responded.

"If you insist." Norman replied with a sarcastic tone, and grin.

With that said, the two of them laughed and stepped inside. Immediately inside, they were greeted by a large rundown looking room. The room had a small, dimly-lit crowd of familiar and unfamiliar faces within it. Mark and Norman quickly began to mingle with the people that they recognized, those ones being mainly from their high school. The ones that they didn't recognize, they introduced themselves to, or were introduced to, and they quickly became acquainted with them as well. This was fun and exciting for the both of them, mainly for Norman, though. He loved to meet new people, hang out with friends, and socialize just about anything and everything. From the very beginning he had always been a "people person," which, considering with what he had planned to do with his life, was a good thing.

As with most boys his age, Norman also really, really liked girls, and for some time, unknown to anyone, he'd had a small, crush on a certain one. Her name was Katrina. Katrina was really, really pretty, and she went to Norman's school. He often thought about her, and what it would be like to get to know her. Most every time he saw Katrina, Norman would get butterflies in his stomach, his heart would feel like it was doing flips, and he could never muster up the courage to talk to her. Usually when he saw her, and if she saw him looking to her, she would smile a pretty smile. But Norman being shy towards her, he would slightly blush and quickly look away. Why he did this, Norman had no clue. Deep down inside, he knew all he had to do was approach Katrina, and say, "Hi."

At one point in time, after inwardly arguing with himself about it, Norman made up his mind. He decided that the next time he saw her, that's exactly what he was gonna do. No nervous stomach, or flipping-heart was going to stop him. He was going to take the first step, and talk to her, or at least say, "Hi."

As it turns out, Norman's inner struggle was all for nothing. He didn't have to approach Katrina first. She showed up at the party and approached him. She stepped into the warehouse with a small group of people, and within just a few seconds of looking around, she spotted Norman. He was talking to a couple of friends, and didn't notice her. Katrina obviously liked Norman as well. She smiled, got goose-bumps, and immediately made her way to him. Neither one of them had a clue that they would both be at the party, and Norman was just as surprised to see her as she was to see him. She stepped up from behind Norman, tapped him on the shoulder, stood next to him, and said with a pretty, wide smile,

"Hi, Norman."

Startled to see that it was, Katrina, Norman's stomach did a quick flip, and he replied,

"Um, hi... uh, what, uh... what are you doing here?"

"Oh, I'm just hanging out." Katrina simply responded, and asked, "You?"

"I'm just hanging out, too." Norman replied, "Came with my buddy, Mark. We were just out riding around, and heard about what was going on here. So, we figured we'd just stop by for a few. Um, you know, just to see what was going on, and stuff."

"Cool." Katrina responded, and asked with another pretty smile, "So, you wanna take a quick walk outside?"

"Um, sure." Norman replied.

Katrina smiled, said, "Great," and walked off.

Norman followed her, and the two of them made their way outside.

Once outside, they walked part-way around the building, and stopped. Katrina had a lighter and some rolled-up-pot, which she pulled from out of one of her pockets, and lit up. She puffed on it, then offered Norman some.

In a real quick flash of time in his mind, Norman momentarily thought about it. He thought about all of the times his parents had talked to him, and warned him about the dangers of doing, using, and abusing street-drugs. From the very day that Norman was old enough to understand, his, mom, dad, and family, had always tried to instill in him the importance of sobriety, living above the influence, and to always steer clear of people that his dad had termed as, "drug-infested losers."

"These people are no good for you. They live in a total different reality. Nothing good ever comes from street drugs, and all they will ever do is bring you down with them. You are gifted, and don't throw it away." His dad had always said.

Norman had always listened, and for the most part, had seemed to have understood. But, as things go with most teens, and most people, Norman really liked Katrina, and though she appeared to liked him as well. He thought by trying the pot, just this one time, that it would impress her, and she would like him even more. So, Norman tried it, and nearly in an instant, everything that had ever been instilled in him quickly went out the window; kept on going, and never came back.

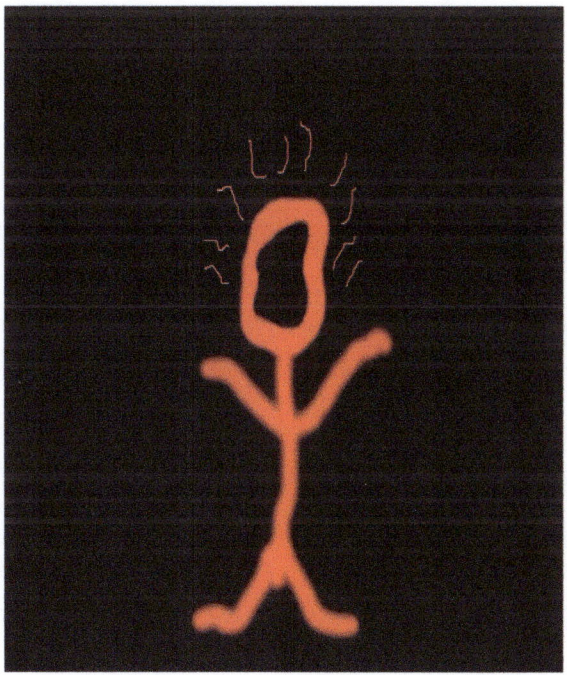

Norman felt silly, fuzzy, and like he was floating around. He was what some call "High." Now, how could a chemical that doesn't belong in one's body, causes the brain to malfunction, destroys cells, and brings it down be called "High?" Seriously, how is that being high, or getting high? Are you standing on a tall building, riding in a plane, helicopter, climbing a tree, living in a tree house, or something similar when you consume, inhale, or ingest? It seems to me that after taking that garbage, or willfully bringing any other similar garbage into your system, you would be in, "Low-malfunctioning-cell-destroyer-mode!" **Not, "High!"**

Unfortunately, for Norman, his parents, his close family, once-time friends, and the whole planet, though as strange as it was, he liked the way he felt, and continued to smoke pot. For the next 5 years, Norman used pot, experimented with other kinds of street drugs, and continued to surround himself with drug-infested losers. This unforeseeable change would have a profound impact on him, his family, and his life to come.

All because of that one brief moment in time, and a very, very bad choice, Norman unintentionally stepped off his path, and turned into a completely different person. His life never went the way it was meant to. The people of Earth, never got to hear his music, and Norman never cared, nor did he know the difference.

This is one of the many reasons street drugs are a very dangerous, dangerous thing for anyone to do, regardless of who you are. People who use, abuse, and become an addict have a very high potential to cause a lot of terrible things to happen, and for teens, they are twice as dangerous, and terrible things are twice as likely to happen.

When teens, or young people experiment/use, they are putting themselves at great risk of never becoming who they were meant to be, and ever fully blossoming into a completely functioning, productive, human being.

You see, for most of us, our brains, and bodies (sometime between the ages of 10 and 12) start a very special stage of development, and for some, this development sometimes isn't fully complete until the age of 25. This is just one of many crucial stages for us. But it is a very crucial stage, and time, because, this time period is when the chemical neurons in our brains go through a major change. They start to really grow, and begin the precise connections that will eventually fully form our personalities into what we'll become. Just like the deep, growing roots of a well-nourished and properly pruned tree. One that will stand tall and grow strong for years to come. Our brains during this stage, when well-nourished and properly pruned, will also grow deep roots, form strong connections, and stay tough for years to come. But if one small thing gets in the way, then these connections can, and will most definitely, grow, become weak, and connect in different ways. In ways they were never meant to be, ultimately altering one's personality, and possibly forever changing their destiny, as they did with Norman. The first time he took a puff, his neurons began to grow and connect in ways they were never meant to, and because for the next 5 years he kept using and abusing street drugs, the neuron connections continued to form improperly.

Example: 1. The chemical compounds in most drugs bind to developing neurons. They alter their growth, strength, and path, instead of them growing, branching out, becoming strong, making tight connections, and fully blooming into this:

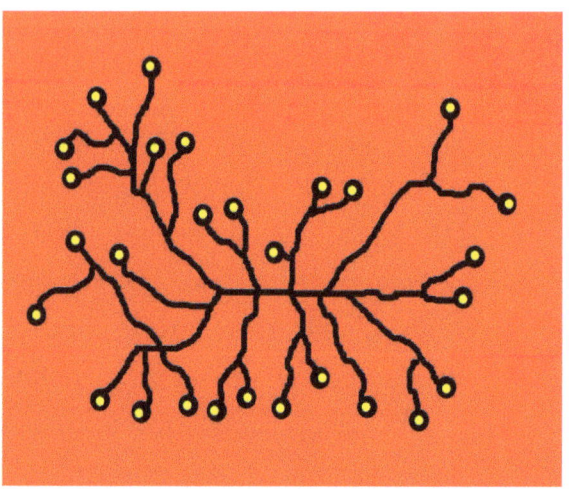

Example: 2. They slowed in growing, became weak, slightly branched out, made a few loose connections, and looked more like this:

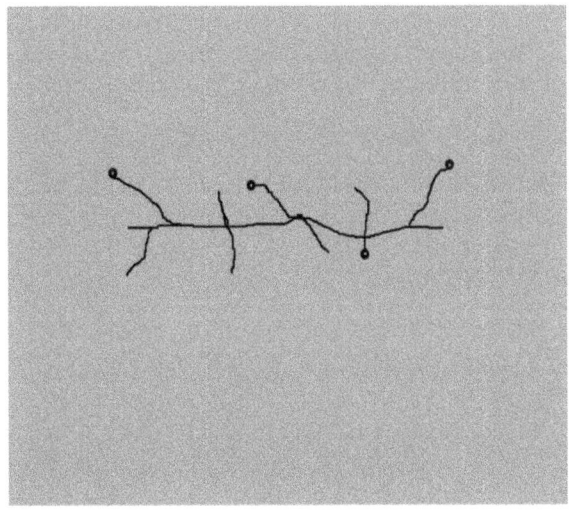

Norman was never the same again. He was no longer pleasant to be around. He constantly back talked his parents, close family, and most adults. He also defied his parents, his teachers, and anyone else who had tried to set him straight. Norman had a really, really big problem. He became a know-it-all, who really knew nothing about anything at all. He was very self-centered, and didn't seem to care about anything anymore. He didn't even care about his drums, or music. His behavior got bad. Terribly bad. In fact, it got so bad that Norman was thrown out of school numerous times, and was eventually expelled. He never graduated, and he didn't care.

There was a couple of times he had gotten into trouble with the law as well. Once was for selling drugs, and the other was for stealing money. Sadly, Norman stole some money from an elderly neighbor that he used to help with yard work, and simple household chores. The neighbor, who had watched Norman grow up and considered him to be a good friend, was very confused and upset about that ordeal. He really couldn't understand what had gotten into Norman. As did everyone else that was once close to him.

Eventually, because Norman's behavior continued, his parents, as heartbroken and saddened as they were, tossed him out and gave up on him. That happened one evening when they tried to confront him about his drug problem. They had done this many times before. But this time they gave him an ultimatum, which Norman didn't want to hear. From his standpoint, they were the ones that were wrong, and they had the problem, not him. So instead of listening, Norman became extremely violent, viciously turned on his parents, and tried to fistfight his dad, which his dad quickly diffused.

Once things were settled down, Norman's mother walked off from the incident crying, and Norman was made to leave.

After, Norman's dad allowed him to grab some of his things together, and, Norman was gone, his dad also cried. He and Norman's mom held each other tight, and cried together.

They truly felt like they had just lost something that was very special to them, and indeed they did. Their son, whom they loved so much, and had the pleasure of raising, became what they had tried their best and so very, very hard to prevent: another young drug casualty.

7

Throughout the next few years of his life, Norman never really did much of anything. He bounced around a lot. Stayed on and off with numerous different friends. Did a lot of odd jobs, and consistently surrounded himself with drug-infested losers. His future wasn't looking too bright, and he wasn't going anywhere. All of his good friends had ditched him. He very rarely spoke to his parents, or what was once his close family. The girl he had liked so much, Katrina, didn't even want anything to do with him. Just in the nick of time, she managed to clean herself up, and never touched drugs again. Norman didn't, though. He didn't see that he had a problem, nor did he care. He was too far gone, and the way he saw it, it was everyone else that had the problem, not him. This was sad, because Norman, as we all are, was meant to be something special, and that something special never happened.

On his 21st birthday, Norman went to a house party with a couple of loser friends to celebrate. Later in the evening, overly intoxicated, and totally confused about where he was, Norman stumbled out of the house, down a street, accidentally into traffic, and was struck by a car. He was killed instantly. His parents got the news within a few hours, and sadly, two days later, Norman was buried.

Placed carefully in his hands by Norman's mom and dad, were a pair of shiny drumsticks with his name and a few words engraved on them. They said,

"Norman Lee Brown. His sticks were strong. His beat was true. The wind will always carry the sound of your drums. We love you, and we'll surely miss you."

Tearfully that day, his family said, "Goodbye." But they always remembered Norman, and they would always smile a warm smile when they thought of the things he had done. That was before the sickness that had unfortunately fallen upon him, came painfully crashing in.

Sometime later it was heard, that when Norman stumbled out of the house, he mumbled,"

"I wanna go home and be with my mom and dad."

The end…

www.davidswarbrick.webs.com

Author Bio

David Swarbrick is a full-time writer and a part-time theoretical physicist. He lives in a small house on the coast of Lake Huron with his wife and son. In his spare time he creates music and studies astronomy.

www.davidswarbrick.webs.com

Author's Books

Happy Root Beer

Every day boys and girls come into the store to buy Happy Root Beer. One day, all the root beer bottles were all bought up. Yet, nobody seems to want to buy Mr. Root Beer. This makes him really sad. Who will come along and help him solve his problem? Join new author David Swarbrick in helping Mr. Root Beer find a new friend to help overcome his loneliness

The Final Breakdown

"Inside this book you will find three short tantalizing stories that are written in the imaginative way that no other author besides David could write them.

Thank you and please enjoy."

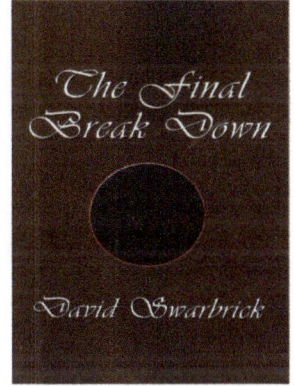

Twenty Goofy Gumballs

One day after earning his allowance, Tommy wanted to spend it on gumballs. So his family walked to the corner store and quickly found themselves falling into a silly adventure of collecting and counting. Join author, David E. Swarbrick, Tommy, and his family in an amazing adventure of collecting and counting...

Peggy's Play House

"Peggy's Play House, a story told by the sun, the moon, the clouds and stars, and even a mouse. It is such a wonderful place to play. Won't you come and read along while we share a warm wonderful day?"

"Oh Yay! We're all going to Peggy's Play House to play!"

The Journey To Eden

"4,000 years ago an elder chief named Walking Tall, who lived in a different galaxy on a large and far away planet, sat at a sacred fire with his young grandson and told him an amazing story of love and triumph that began a long, long time ago.

Join Walking Tall and his grandson, Stalking Crow, by the sacred fire and listen while the twisting story of a warriors journey to Eden unfolds."

"Captain on the bridge!"

"Commander Report!"

"Aye, Sir, we have two unidentified vessels holding position over our bow."

"So let me guess, you're the biblical devil that I've read about?"

"The diary devise was found on Mars wasn't it?"

A New Beginning

Mark Morgan is young, smart, handsome, and also very wealthy. His writing career is beginning to blossom, and it's starting to take him to the places in life that he had always wanted to go. His ravishing wife Kara is pregnant, and going to eventually give birth to the little girl Mark had always wanted; everything is going great for him. But as life always is with most everyone, when things are going good, an unexpected tragedy takes place and disrupts Mark's happiness. It happens to him not once, but twice. He becomes mentally ill, severely heartbroken from the tragic events, and seeks professional help from a well-known and locally renowned psychologist named Susan Downs. Mark eventually becomes really close to her and falls in love with her. But in the end she has a really big, and totally shocking surprise for him. The surprise ends with her death, and the rescue of Marks next wife, who eventually bares him two children. Mark also has a surprise. But this one's for the reader, and it's a secret that he has been able to keep quiet his whole life. What is it about him that's so different? No one but his mother knows. Susan suspected all along there was something about him that was, or something that he was intently hiding. In the end she never finds out, but the reader does, and so will you. So, stick around, keep reading, find out in the end what Mark's big secret is, and see what course it sets for humanity.

www.ingramcontent.com/pod-product-compliance
Lightning Source LLC
Chambersburg PA
CBHW061226070526
44584CB00029B/4006